Bond
No.1 for exam success

SATs Skills

Spelling and Vocabulary Workbook

9–10 years

OXFORD
UNIVERSITY PRESS

Great Clarendon Street, Oxford, OX2 6DP, United Kingdom

Oxford University Press is a department of the University of Oxford.
It furthers the University's objective of excellence in research, scholarship,
and education by publishing worldwide. Oxford is a registered trade mark
of Oxford University Press in the UK and in certain other countries

British Library Cataloguing in Publication Data
Data available

978-0-19-274653-5

15

Paper used in the production of this book is a natural, recyclable product
made from wood grown in sustainable forests. The manufacturing process
conforms to the environmental regulations of the country of origin.

Printed in China

Acknowledgements

Cover illustrations: Lo Cole

Although we have made every effort to trace and contact all copyright
holders before publication this has not been possible in all cases.
If notified, the publisher will rectify any errors or omissions at the
earliest opportunity.

Links to third party websites are provided by Oxford in good faith and for
information only. Oxford disclaims any responsibility for the materials
contained in any third party website referenced in this work.

Unit 1

A All of your words are hidden in the word search. They go across and down, but not diagonally. Find your words and then find the leftover letters. What do the leftover letters spell out? [17]

W	C	D	I	S	E	A	S	E	H
O	H	E	X	C	E	E	D	A	E
B	E	A	K	E	R	R	D	G	A
E	A	T	H	R	E	A	T	L	L
A	P	H	E	A	V	E	N	E	T
K	F	E	A	T	H	E	R	W	H
G	L	E	A	M	I	N	G	H	Y
H	E	A	T	H	E	R	S	E	W
S	P	E	A	K	E	R	I	A	T
H	W	E	A	K	E	N	E	T	A

B Remove one letter from each of the following words to make a new word. [8]

1 beaker _____

2 feather _____

3 heaven _____

4 weaken _____

5 cheap _____

6 healthy _____

7 wheat _____

8 threat _____

C Replace the first letter of each of the following words to make a new word. [6]

1 beak _____

2 death _____

3 healthy _____

4 beaker _____

5 feather _____

6 wheat _____

beak

beaker

cheap

death

disease

eagle

exceed

feather

gleaming

healthy

heather

heaven

speaker

threat

weaken

wheat

31

Unit 1

art

ban

bud

cob

con

dot

dye

fee

gap

gum

hum

ivy

shy

sty

tin

wry

30

D Write the three-letter words that are hidden in these longer words. [16]

1   dehumanise   _____   9   delighting   _____

2   martyrs   _____   10   argument   _____

3   anecdotal   _____   11   dowry   _____

4   budgerigar   _____   12   midyear   _____

5   polystyrene   _____   13   turban   _____

6   coffeepot   _____   14   cobwebs   _____

7   archdeacons   _____   15   megaphone   _____

8   privy   _____   16   squashy   _____

E Place one of your words in each space below, using each word only once. [14]

1–2   Find two words to which we can we add an 'a' to make another word.
_____ and _____

3–4   Find two words to which we can we add a 'p' to make another word.
_____ and _____

5–6   Find two words to which we can we add an 'e' to make another word.
_____ and _____

7–8   Find two words to which we can add a 't' to make another word.
_____ and _____

9–10   Find two words to which we can add an 's' to make another word.
_____ and _____

11   Find a word to which we can add an 'a' and an 'n' to make another word.

_____

12   Find a word to which we can add an 'o' and an 'r' to make another word.

_____

13   Find a word to which we can add an 'l' to make another word.

_____

14   Find a word to which we can add a 'd' to make another word.

_____

F) All of your words are hidden in the word search. They go across and down, but not diagonally. Find your words and then find the leftover letters. What do the leftover letters spell out? [17]

N	S	T	R	E	N	G	T	H
I	T	H	F	E	T	C	H	E
N	S	E	B	A	T	H	W	O
T	R	P	I	D	D	U	L	W
H	H	I	R	S	C	R	A	C
B	U	N	C	H	P	C	T	A
M	N	C	H	A	T	H	C	L
O	C	H	L	L	H	U	H	T
T	H	U	T	C	H	S	E	H
H	L	E	N	G	T	H	T	H
O	R	C	W	I	D	T	H	H

G) An antonym is a word that is opposite in meaning to another. Which of your words are antonyms for these words? [3]

1 take _____   3 poverty _____

2 weakness _____

H) A synonym is a word that is similar in meaning to another. Which of your words are synonyms for these words? [8]

1 nip _____   5 riches _____

2 clump _____   6 deepness _____

3 power _____   7 instinct _____

4 cage _____   8 chapel _____

bath

birch

bunch

church

depth

fetch

hunch

hutch

latch

length

moth

ninth

pinch

strength

wealth

width

28

Unit 1

ape

bore

cave

cove

drake

fate

frame

kite

lace

rake

rate

spoke

tape

tone

tune

wove

26

(I) Place one of your words in each space so that the sentences make sense. [16]

1 _____ is an intricate pattern or decorative fabric.

2 Another word for ribbon is _____ .

3 A songwriter sets words to a _____ .

4 Around the coast we find a _____ which is a sheltered bay.

5 An _____ is an animal.

6 _____ means luck or fortune.

7 A border around a photograph or picture is called a _____ .

8 The past tense of speak is _____ .

9 The _____ is the cost or speed of something.

10 A _____ is a hollow or tunnel in a cliff, hill or mountainside.

11 On a windy day it is great fun to fly a _____ .

12 To _____ is to drill a hole.

13 The past tense of weave is _____ .

14 The word _____ means a shade, or a musical sound or to shape up.

15 A male duck is called a _____ .

16 A _____ is a gardening tool.

(J) Change the first letter in each of the following words to make a new word. [10]

Example: bore _____core_____

1 cave _____ 6 cove _____

2 fate _____ 7 kite _____

3 lace _____ 8 rake _____

4 rate _____ 9 tape _____

5 tone _____ 10 wove _____

Unit 2

(A) All of your words are hidden in the word search. They go across and down but not diagonally. Find your words and then find the leftover letters. What do the leftover letters spell out? [17]

_____

G	B	A	N	A	N	A	W	O	S
R	A	S	P	B	E	R	R	Y	T
A	P	R	I	C	O	T	R	P	R
P	I	N	E	A	P	P	L	E	A
E	D	S	T	O	H	A	E	A	W
F	C	H	E	R	R	Y	M	C	B
R	H	U	B	A	R	B	O	H	E
U	T	A	R	N	E	F	N	R	R
I	M	A	N	G	O	U	I	T	R
T	L	I	M	E	P	L	U	M	Y
A	P	P	L	E	G	R	A	P	E

(B) Write the three-letter words that are hidden in these words. [10]

1 apricot _____

2 banana _____

3 cherry _____

4 grapefruit _____

5 mango _____

6 orange _____

7 peach _____

8 pineapple _____

9 rhubarb _____

10 strawberry _____

Word list (Unit 2):

apple

apricot

banana

cherry

grape

grapefruit

lemon

lime

mango

orange

peach

pineapple

plum

raspberry

rhubarb

strawberry

💡 **Helpful Hint**

Some fruits make use of common spelling strings. If you can spell 'cherry' you can spell all of the 'berry' words (cranberry, strawberry, blueberry) and the plural of this ('cherries') gives you the same spelling string as all of the plural 'berries'.

27

Unit 2

acorn

armour

bandage

bandit

bargain

bathe

birthday

bitten

blackbird

bluebell

buttercup

butterflies

cupcake

damage

daydream

download

25

(c) Fill in the grid with all of your words, using the clues to help you. [16]

Across

1 To physically harm
3 A knight's protective clothing
5 Pretty insects
7 A garden bird
10 A tasty treat
11 To be gnawed
12 To go into a trance
13 A day to celebrate your age

Down

1 To get online information
2 A wildflower
3 The fruit of an oak tree
4 Something bought cheaply
6 To soak
7 A spring flower
8 Found in a first-aid kit
9 A thief or robber

(D) Using the words below, add another word to create new, longer words. [9]

Example: day*time*, day*break*, day*light*

1 a_____, a_____, a_____

2 black_____, black_____, black_____

3 arm_____, arm_____, arm_____

💡 **Helpful Hint**

Compound words are made up of two or more smaller words. This can help you with your spellings, especially when the compound word does not sound like its component words.

Unit 2

E Fill in the grid with all of your words. The first letter of each word has been given to help you. [16]

F Which of your words fit the descriptions below? [16]

1 Who works with play scripts? _____

2 Who flies an aeroplane? _____

3 Who looks after children? _____

4 Who works with paint? _____

5 Who works in an office? _____

6 Who creates meals? _____

7 Who looks after our teeth? _____

8 Who designs buildings? _____

9 Who researches new discoveries? _____

10 Who works in a museum? _____

11 Who works in a church? _____

12 Who do we visit if we are ill? _____

13 Who catches criminals? _____

14 Who works with books? _____

15 Who works on hospital wards? _____

16 Who plays an instrument? _____

actor

architect

artist

chef

curator

dentist

doctor

librarian

musician

nanny

nurse

pilot

police

priest

scientist

secretary

32

amuse

bike

blade

blame

complete

crime

describe

dome

entire

file

flame

flute

glide

globe

primrose

strange

33

(G) All of your words fit into the grid. Work out which number represents each letter to solve the puzzle. [17]

	4																
A	B	C	D	E	F	G	I	K	L	M	N	O	P	R	S	T	U

Crossword grid (numbers):

4   6
26 5 25 7   13
16   22   19
6   7   13 26
16   9   5
7   1   12 25 1 13
17 7 10 19 13   13   4 18
3   3   13 3
9 5 25 7 5 16 19 13   25
17   12   5
4 18   12 1 17 7 13
1 21 1 25 6 13   10
4 1 17 7 13   3
6   21 1 16 4 13
13

(H) Which of your words are synonyms for these words? [10]

1 entertain _____
2 slide _____
3 offence _____
4 document _____
5 eerie _____

6 accuse _____
7 finish _____
8 whole _____
9 earth _____
10 blaze _____

(I) Which of your words are antonyms for these words? [6]

1 ordinary _____
2 begin _____
3 none _____

4 stumble _____
5 bore _____
6 forgive _____

Unit 3

(A) All of your words fit into the grid. Work out which number represents each letter to solve the puzzle. [20]

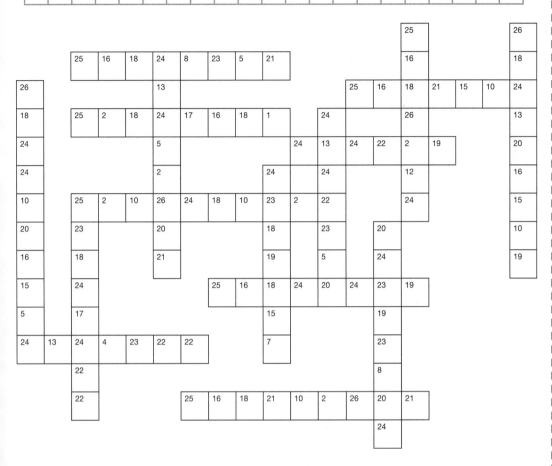

A	B	C	D	E	F	G	H	I	K	L	M	N	O	R	S	T	U	V	W	Y
			24																	

(B) Divide the words from your list into their two component words. [15]

Example: eardrum ___ear___ + ___drum___

1 _____ + _____   9 _____ + _____

2 _____ + _____   10 _____ + _____

3 _____ + _____   11 _____ + _____

4 _____ + _____   12 _____ + _____

5 _____ + _____   13 _____ + _____

6 _____ + _____   14 _____ + _____

7 _____ + _____   15 _____ + _____

8 _____ + _____

Unit 3

eardrum

eyeball

eyelash

eyelid

eyesight

farewell

fingernail

firework

forecast

forehead

forgive

fortnight

fortune

greenhouse

greyhound

headache

35

Unit 3

believe

brief

ceiling

chief

deceive

eerie

eighth

either

experience

mischief

niece

pierce

receipt

relieved

replied

weird

22

C Place one of your words in each space so that the sentences make sense. [16]

1 Camping was a brilliant _____ as we were so close to nature.

2 My auntie says that I am her favourite _____ .

3 It was so _____ seeing my teacher on holiday in the same hotel!

4 The woods at night became an _____ place to be.

5 The kitten caused _____ by unravelling the ball of wool.

6 The _____ engineer was in charge of five other engineers.

7 I returned the broken crockery to the shop as I had the _____ .

8 I do _____ that reading books widens our vocabulary.

9 The pupils were asked to answer _____ question one or question two.

10 Nobody _____ when we knocked on the door.

11 The boy tried to _____ the teacher, but the teacher had the results.

12 Unfortunately, out of eight pupils, the boy came _____ .

13 We all took a _____ break before returning to the meeting room.

14 The decorator painted the _____ white to lighten the room.

15 I was _____ when I had my results and knew that my leg wasn't broken.

16 You might _____ the balloon if you put it near the rose bush.

D Which of your words are synonyms for each of these words? [6]

1 naughtiness _____   4 lie   _____

2 trust   _____   5 short   _____

3 main   _____   6 answered   _____

 Helpful Hint

The famous reminder for spelling 'ie' and 'ei' words is: I before E except after C but some WEIRD words are DISAGREEING so don't forget EITHER or NEITHER!

Unit 3

E Use a line to join the adult animal names to the baby animal names. [16]

cow	deer	dog	duck	ferret	fish	fox	frog

calf   chick   cub   cygnet   duckling

fawn   foal   fry   gosling   kid   kit

lamb   owlet   piglet   puppy   tadpole

goat	goose	hen	horse	pig	owl	sheep	swan

F Some of these words can have one letter added to make a new word. Write the new word below. [4]

Example: chick + s = _chicks_

1   cub + e = _____   3   kid + n = _____

2   fry + a = _____   4   kit + e = _____

G Some of these words can have the first letter removed and another added to make a new word. Write the new word below. [8]

Example: duckling _buckling_

1   chick _____   5   foal _____

2   cub _____   6   fry _____

3   calf _____   7   kid _____

4   fawn _____   8   kit _____

💡 **Helpful Hint**
The ending 'let' is used for many words to describe something small. Can you think of other words that end in 'let' that follow this pattern?

_____ _____ _____

calf

chick

cub

cygnet

duckling

fawn

foal

fry

gosling

kid

kit

lamb

owlet

piglet

puppy

tadpole

28

admit

adult

alert

fight

float

garnet

grant

habit

habitat

inspect

instant

instruct

insult

reject

sprint

toilet

31

(H) All of your words are hidden in the word search. They go across and down but not diagonally. Find your words and then find the leftover letters. What do the leftover letters spell out? [17]

_____

H	A	B	I	T	A	T	T	I	F
A	D	M	I	T	D	H	G	N	I
B	E	S	E	A	U	L	A	S	G
I	L	E	N	A	L	E	R	T	H
T	O	I	L	E	T	D	N	A	T
G	I	N	S	U	L	T	E	N	F
R	I	N	S	P	E	C	T	T	L
A	I	N	S	T	R	U	C	T	O
N	R	E	J	E	C	T	I	N	A
T	S	P	R	I	N	T	A	T	T

(I) Which of your words are antonyms for these words? [6]

1 sink _____

2 deny _____

3 accept _____

4 praise _____

5 sleepy _____

6 child _____

(J) Which of your words are synonyms for these words? [8]

1 run _____

2 teach _____

3 routine _____

4 mature _____

5 environment _____

6 awake _____

7 argue _____

8 check _____

Recap

Unit 4

(A) Fill in the grid with all of your words, using the clues to help you. [16]

Across

2 One person
3 A game played on horseback
4 Information
5 A large country
7 Seating for more than one person
10 Two people
11 A sound that repeats
12 A place that shows films
14 Baggage
15 Region

Down

1 A vegetable
2 Fizzy water
6 Three people
8 A tiny insect
9 A chocolate drink
13 A period of time

(B) Write the plurals of these words. [12]

1 area _____
2 cargo _____
3 cinema _____
4 duo _____
5 echo _____
6 era _____

7 flea _____
8 potato _____
9 soda _____
10 sofa _____
11 solo _____
12 trio _____

 Helpful Hint

The vowel that is most commonly used to end English words is an 'e'.
Words from other languages often end in other vowels. Can you find out
where the words in the list on this page originate from?

area

cargo

China

cinema

cocoa

data

duo

echo

era

flea

polo

potato

soda

sofa

solo

trio

28

Unit 4

Bond SATs Skills Spelling and Vocabulary 9–10

bride

bridle

eight

faction

fraction

haze

hazel

height

learn

learnt

print

reign

rein

sprint

vanish

varnish

20

C Place one of your words in each space so that the sentences make sense. [16]

1   We have a _____ tree in our garden.

2   A _____ is the long strap attached to the horse's bit.

3   I completed my homework but did not get chance to _____ it out.

4   Soaking the material in bleach made the stain _____ overnight.

5   The _____ path was used by many horses.

6   I need to _____ my multiplication tables for a test next week.

7   There were _____ children in the group.

8   A quarter is a _____ meaning one out of four.

9   The runner managed to _____ for the last part of the race.

10 I have _____ how to ride my bike without stabilisers.

11 The _____ and groom were married last week.

12 The islands could just be seen below the _____ of cloud and sunlight.

13 One splinter group, or _____ , joined the debate with an alternative view.

14 Queen Victoria's _____ was between 1837 and 1901.

15 If we _____ the wood it will be much more durable.

16 The _____ of the tree was perfect for nesting owls.

D Remove one letter from each of the following words to make a new word. [4]

1   learn   _____   3   print   _____

2   faction   _____   4   bride   _____

💡 **Helpful Hint**

Can you think of other pairs of words where the first word can have a letter added to make another word? You might be surprised how many you can find!

_____ _____ _____

16

E) Fill in the grid with all of your words. The first letter of each word has been given to help you. [16]

announce

annoyed

attend

banner

bitter

burrow

butter

cotton

cuddle

effect

fluffy

followed

kettle

summer

teddies

village

F) Write each of your words out, breaking them into their syllables. [16]

1 _____   9 _____

2 _____   10 _____

3 _____   11 _____

4 _____   12 _____

5 _____   13 _____

6 _____   14 _____

7 _____   15 _____

8 _____   16 _____

 Helpful Hint

These words all have double consonants in them. If we break each word into syllables, the break will fall between the two double letters. **Example:** 'an-noyed'. This is a good way of remembering how to spell them.

32

caught

court

currant

current

guessed

guest

heard

herd

idle

idol

morning

mourning

stationary

stationery

vain

vein

26

(G) A homophone is a word that sounds the same as another word but has a different spelling and a different meaning. Draw a line to match these homophones with their definitions. [16]

1	caught	Carries our blood along
2	court	Between midnight and noon
3	currant	Someone invited into your home
4	current	Where a judge considers evidence
5	guessed	To be lazy
6	guest	The past tense of catch
7	heard	Paper, envelopes, pens and pencils
8	herd	The past tense of hear
9	idle	A dried grape
10	idol	To be bereaved after a death or loss
11	morning	An electrical flow
12	mourning	Formed an answer without knowledge
13	stationary	A group of animals such as cows
14	stationery	To feel overly proud of appearance
15	vain	Not moving
16	vein	An object that is worshipped

(H) Which of your words are antonyms for these words? [4]

1 afternoon _____   3 moving _____

2 busy _____   4 modest _____

(I) Which of your words are synonyms for these words? [6]

1 grieving _____   4 flock _____

2 visitor _____   5 proud _____

3 captured _____   6 modern _____

Unit 5

(A) Fill in the grid with twelve of your words. One letter in each word has been provided as a clue. [12]

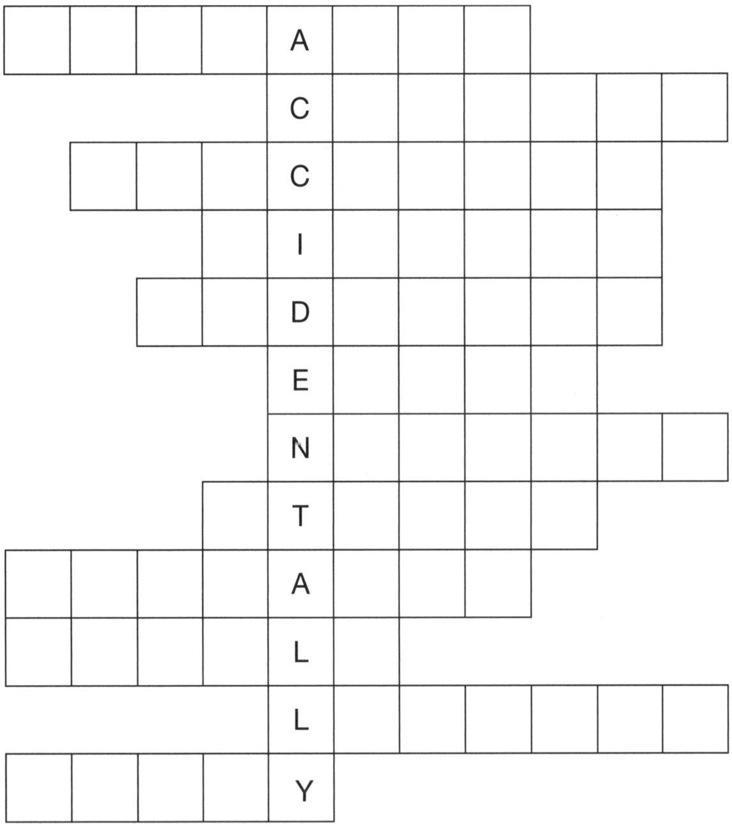

(The grid contains the following clue letters arranged vertically: A, C, C, I, D, E, N, T, A, L, L, Y)

(B) Which of your words are synonyms for these words? [4]

1   really   _____   3   sometimes _____

2   normal   _____   4   likely   _____

(C) Write the following words as adjectives. [3]

Example: actually ____*actual*____

1   probably   _____   3   specially   _____

2   occasionally _____

(D) Write the following words as nouns. [2]

Example: accidentally ____*accident*____

1   beady   _____   2   bubbly   _____

Helpful Hint

Remember this spelling rule to help you when adding a 'y' to the end of a word:
If a word ends in an 'e' that you cannot hear, drop the 'e' and add the 'y'.
Example: 'injure' drops the 'e' to become 'injury'.

accidentally

actually

beady

bubbly

century

essay

ferry

history

injury

library

naughty

occasionally

ordinary

probably

specially

sturdy

21

Unit 5

black

blue

brown

gold

green

grey

indigo

navy

pink

purple

scarlet

silver

tan

turquoise

white

yellow

27

(E) All of your words are hidden in the word search. They go across and down but not diagonally. Find your words and then find the leftover letters. What do the leftover letters spell out? [17]

_____

G	O	L	D	C	O	B	L	U	E
L	P	U	R	P	L	E	O	G	Y
U	R	F	S	I	L	V	E	R	E
G	R	E	E	N	U	L	T	E	L
B	L	A	C	K	W	O	A	Y	L
R	I	N	D	I	G	O	N	R	O
O	S	C	A	R	L	E	T	D	W
W	H	I	T	E	S	N	A	V	Y
N	T	U	R	Q	U	O	I	S	E

(F) Which of your words have these smaller words hidden in them? [10]

1 lack _____   **6** in _____

2 dig _____   **7** an _____

3 row _____   **8** low _____

4 ink _____   **9** old _____

5 car _____   **10** is _____

 Helpful Hint

Now you have some excellent descriptive words to use. Leave 'red' and 'blue' and describe your character as wearing a **scarlet** dress, or describe the sea as **turquoise** with flashes of **navy**. Why not find more descriptive colours to help your writing even more? Write one descriptive sentence that uses some of your new words:

_____

_____

Unit 5

G All of these words have more than one meaning, which means they are homonyms. Which one word fits both definitions in these questions? [16]

1   A fried sliver of potato. Cool.   _____

2   Curiosity. The additional sum awarded for saving money.   _____

3   A mathematical shape. A percussion musical instrument.   _____

4   Leftover remains of a fire. A type of tree.   _____

5   A stand-alone clause. A term of punishment.   _____

6   To rip. The product created when we cry.   _____

7   A flat-bottomed boat. To shove or push.   _____

8   A burgundy, red colour. To abandon.   _____

9   Where we live. To give a lecture or talk.   _____

10   A sharp point. Moving very quickly.   _____

11   A container for petrol or water. A vehicle used by the army.   _____

12   To badly miss somebody or something. An evergreen tree.   _____

13   A bird. Moving with great speed.   _____

14   A sticky, dried fruit. Part of a calendar.   _____

15   A gemstone. A shape.   _____

16   To tap repeatedly. A percussion musical instrument.   _____

H Remove one letter from each of the following words to make a new word. [8]

1   date   _____   5   swift   _____

2   dart   _____   6   tank   _____

3   ash   _____   7   pine   _____

4   tear   _____   8   barge   _____

| address |
| ash |
| barge |
| crisp |
| dart |
| date |
| diamond |
| drum |
| interest |
| maroon |
| pine |
| sentence |
| swift |
| tank |
| tear |
| triangle |

 Helpful Hint

These homonyms can be tricky, but a lot of the time a homonym is a verb and a noun. Think of 'water': I can get a drink of water or I can water my plants. Always ask yourself if the word is an action, a thing or both.

24

Unit 5

connect

flutter

hurry

pillow

rattle

ribbon

rotten

ruffle

shatter

shopper

shopping

shutter

silly

spotty

stripped

summit

30

(I) Find the words that fit the definitions below. [16]

1   Someone who buys things _____

2   Stale or mouldy _____

3   Daft or foolish _____

4   Made bare _____

5   To go quickly _____

6   Purchasing items _____

7   The movement of butterfly wings _____

8   To shake _____

9   A wooden window covering _____

10 Having blotches _____

11 A cushion for a bed _____

12 To join together _____

13 A colourful tape _____

14 To smash into pieces _____

15 A decorative piece of fabric _____

16 The top of a mountain _____

(J) All but one of your words have two syllables. We split the syllable in the middle of the double letters. Write your words divided into syllables. [14]

Example: _____con-nect_____

1 _____   8 _____

2 _____   9 _____

3 _____   10 _____

4 _____   11 _____

5 _____   12 _____

6 _____   13 _____

7 _____   14 _____

↻ Recap

Answers

Worked word searches can be found at the back of this book.

Unit 1

(A) Leftover letters spell: WORDS WITH EA

(B)
1 baker
2 father
3 haven / heave
4 waken
5 heap / chap
6 health
7 heat / what / whet
8 treat

(C)
1 peak, leak, teak, weak
2 heath
3 wealthy
4 weaker
5 heather, weather, leather
6 cheat

(D)
1 hum
2 art
3 dot
4 bud
5 sty
6 fee
7 con
8 ivy
9 tin
10 gum
11 wry
12 dye
13 ban
14 cob
15 gap
16 shy

(E)
1–2 sty (stay), wry (wary)
3–4 art (part), hum (hump)
5–6 Any two of the following: ban (bean, bane), con (cone), gap (gape), tin (tine), sty (stye)
7–8 Any two of the following: art (tart), fee (feet), tin (tint)
9–10 Any two of the following: art (arts), ban (bans), bud (buds), con (cons), fee (fees), gap (gaps), hum (hums)
11 hum (human), sty (nasty)
12 wry (worry), ivy (ivory)
13 fee (feel, flee), tin (lint)
14 Any of the following: fee (feed), ban (band), dye (dyed)

(F) Leftover letters spell: THESE WORDS ALL USE TH OR CH

(G)
1 fetch
2 strength
3 wealth

(H)
1 pinch
2 bunch
3 strength
4 hutch
5 wealth
6 depth
7 hunch
8 church

(I)
1 lace
2 tape
3 tune
4 cove
5 ape
6 fate
7 frame
8 spoke
9 rate
10 cave
11 kite
12 bore
13 wove
14 tone
15 drake
16 rake

(J) Examples include:
1 save / wave / nave
2 date / gate / hate
3 face / pace / race
4 late / mate / rate
5 bone / cone / gone
6 dove / love / wove
7 bite / site / mite
8 bake / sake / cake
9 cape / gape / nape
10 cove / love / dove

Unit 2

(A) Leftover letters spell: WORDS THAT ARE FRUIT

(B)
1 cot
2 ban
3 her
4 ape / rap
5 man
6 ran
7 pea
8 pin
9 bar / hub
10 raw

(C) Across:
1 damage
3 armour
5 butterflies
7 blackbird
10 cupcake
11 bitten
12 daydream
13 birthday

Down:
1 download
2 buttercup
3 acorn
4 bargain
6 bathe
7 bluebell
8 bandage
9 bandit

(D) Longer word examples:
1 ago, awhile, away
2 blackberry, blackboard, blackbird
3 armpit, armhole, armband

(E)

(F)
1 actor
2 pilot
3 nanny
4 artist
5 secretary
6 chef
7 dentist
8 architect
9 scientist
10 curator
11 priest
12 doctor
13 police
14 librarian
15 nurse
16 musician

(G)

1/	4	26	6	13	12	21	25	22	1	7	18	16	9	5	19	3	10
A	B	C	D	E	F	G	I	K	L	M	N	O	P	R	S	T	U

(H)
1 amuse
2 glide
3 crime
4 file
5 strange
6 blame
7 complete
8 entire
9 globe
10 flame

(I)
1 strange
2 complete
3 entire
4 glide
5 amuse
6 blame

Unit 3

(A)

23	4	8	19	24	25	26	20	2	1	22	7	10	16	18	5	21	15	12	17	13
A	B	C	D	E	F	G	H	I	K	L	M	N	O	R	S	T	U	V	W	Y

(B)
1 eye + ball = eyeball
2 eye + lash = eyelash
3 eye + lid = eyelid
4 eye + sight = eyesight
5 fare + well = farewell
6 finger + nail = fingernail
7 fire + work = firework
8 fore + cast = forecast
9 fore + hand = forehand
10 for + give = forgive
11 fort + night = fortnight
12 for + tune = fortune
13 green + house = greenhouse
14 grey + hound = greyhound
15 head + ache = headache

(C)
1 experience
2 niece
3 weird
4 eerie
5 mischief
6 chief
7 receipt
8 believe
9 either
10 replied
11 deceive
12 eighth
13 brief
14 ceiling
15 relieved
16 pierce

(D)
1 mischief
2 believe
3 chief
4 deceive
5 brief
6 replied

(E) In any order:
1 cow – calf
2 deer – fawn
3 dog – puppy
4 duck – duckling
5 ferret – kit
6 fish – fry
7 fox – cub
8 frog – tadpole
9 goat – kid
10 goose – gosling
11 hen – chick
12 horse – foal
13 pig – piglet
14 owl – owlet
15 sheep – lamb
16 swan – cygnet

(F)
1 cube
2 fray
3 kind
4 kite

(G) Examples include:
1 thick
2 tub / rub
3 half
4 lawn / dawn
5 coal / goal
6 cry / dry
7 lid / hid
8 bit / fit

(H) Leftover letters spell: THESE ALL END IN A T

(I) 1 float
2 admit
3 reject

4 insult
5 alert
6 adult

(J) 1 sprint
2 instruct
3 habit
4 adult

5 habitat
6 alert
7 fight
8 inspect

Unit 4

(A) **Across:**
2 solo
3 polo
4 data
5 China
7 sofa
10 duo
11 echo
12 cinema
14 cargo
15 area

Down:
1 potato
2 soda
6 trio
8 flea
9 cocoa
13 era

(B) 1 areas
2 cargoes / cargos
3 cinemas
4 duos
5 echoes
6 eras

7 fleas
8 potatoes
9 sodas
10 sofas
11 solos
12 trios

(C) 1 hazel
2 rein
3 print
4 vanish

5 bridle
6 learn
7 eight
8 fraction

9 sprint
10 learnt
11 bride
12 haze

13 faction
14 reign
15 varnish
16 height

(D) 1 lean   2 action   3 pint   4 ride

(E)

```
                              F L U F F Y
              B               O
              A         C     L
          A N N O Y E D       L
          T   E     D   B U T T E R   V I L L A G E
          T   N     D             E   N
          I   N     L             N   D
        T E D D I E S   B U R R O W
          E         F
          R         F   C O T T O N
                    E                 U
                    C         S U M M E R
              K E T T L E
```

Note: BUTTER and BITTER could also be placed the other way around.

(F) **In any order:**

1 an-nounce
2 an-noyed
3 at-tend
4 ban-ner
5 bit-ter
6 bur-row

7 but-ter
8 cot-ton
9 cud-dle
10 ef-fect
11 fluf-fy
12 fol-lowed

13 ket-tle
14 sum-mer
15 vil-lage
16 ted-dies

(G) 1 caught – the past tense of catch
2 court – where a judge considers evidence
3 currant – a dried grape
4 current – an electrical flow
5 guessed – formed an answer without knowledge
6 guest – someone invited into your home
7 heard – the past tense of hear
8 herd – a group of animals such as cows
9 idle – to be lazy
10 idol – an object that is worshipped
11 morning – between midnight and noon
12 mourning – to be bereaved after a death or loss
13 stationary – not moving
14 stationery – paper, envelopes, pens and pencils
15 vain – to feel overly proud of appearance
16 vein – carries along our blood

(H) 1 morning   2 idle   3 stationary   4 vain

(I) 1 mourning
2 guest
3 caught

4 herd
5 vain
6 current

Unit 5

(A)

```
P R O B A B L Y
        C E N T U R Y
S P E C I A L L Y
        H I S T O R Y
    O R D I N A R Y
        E S S A Y
        N A U G H T Y
        S T U R D Y
A C T U A L L Y
B U B B L Y
        L I B R A R Y
B E A D Y
```

(B) 1 actually
2 ordinary

3 occasionally
4 probably

(C) 1 probable   2 occasional   3 special

(D) 1 bead   2 bubble

(E) **Leftover letters spell:** COLOURFUL WORDS

(F) 1 black
2 indigo
3 brown
4 pink
5 scarlet

6 indigo / pink
7 tan
8 yellow
9 gold
10 tuquoise

(G) 1 crisp
2 interest
3 triangle
4 ash
5 sentence
6 tear
7 barge
8 maroon

9 address
10 dart
11 tank
12 pine
13 swift
14 date
15 diamond
16 drum

(H) 1 ate   3 as   5 sift   7 pin
2 art   4 ear / tar   6 tan   8 bare

(I) 1 shopper
2 rotten
3 silly
4 stripped
5 hurry
6 shopping
7 flutter
8 rattle

9 shutter
10 spotty
11 pillow
12 connect
13 ribbon
14 shatter
15 ruffle
16 summit

(J) 1 flut-ter
2 hur-ry
3 pil-low
4 rat-tle
5 rib-bon
6 rot-ten
7 ruf-fle

8 shat-ter
9 shop-per
10 shop-ping
11 shut-ter
12 sil-ly
13 spot-ty
14 sum-mit

Unit 6

(A) 1 sun + flower
2 sun + light
3 sun + shine
4 sup + ply
5 sup + port
6 tab + let
7 tar + get
8 tea + cup

9 tea + pot
10 tea + spoon
11 thin + king
12 toad + stool
13 toe + nail
14 trap + door
15 tea + time

(B) 1 teapot, teacup
2 sunflower, supply, sunlight
3 teaspoon
4 toadstool, trapdoor, teatime

(C) 1 door   2 sheet   3 brood   4 feel

Ⓓ 1 c e k o o r
   2 g l m o o y
   3 e e g r t
   4 e e e l s v
   5 f h i l o o s

Ⓔ 1 cooker
   2 coop
   3 sleeve
   4 deer
   5 foolish
   6 indoors
   7 broom
   8 blood
   9 gloomy
   10 greet
   11 breed
   12 fleece

Ⓕ **In any order:**
   1 snowball
   2 moonlight
   3 passport
   4 outlaw
   5 rainbow
   6 outstanding
   7 overheard
   8 package
   9 password
   10 railway
   11 overall
   12 raincoat
   13 snowdrop
   14 overtake
   15 snowflake
   16 outside

Ⓖ **Prepositions:**
   outstanding, overheard,
   overall, overtake, outside
   Nature: snowball, rainbow,
   raincoat, snowdrop,
   snowflake

   Other: passport, railway,
   password

Ⓗ 1 possession
   2 business
   3 particular
   4 guide
   5 separate
   6 argue
   7 especially
   8 peculiar
   9 thought
   10 definite

Ⓘ
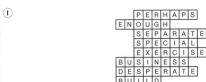

Unit 7

Ⓐ
26	20	2	10	8	14	7	21	25	19	9	17	16	4	22	13	11	23	24
A	B	D	E	G	H	I	K	L	M	N	O	P	R	S	T	U	W	X

Ⓑ 1 disappear
   2 dawn
   3 dusk
   4 impossible

Ⓒ 1 east
   2 impossible
   3 wane
   4 south
   5 dusk
   6 popular

Ⓓ
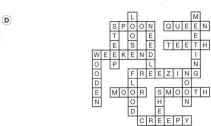

Note: STEEP and SHEET could also be placed the other way around.

Ⓔ **In any order:**
   1 **'OO' sound:** smooth, spoon, loose
   2 **'E' sound:** needle, queen, sheet, steep, teeth, weekend, creepy, freezing
   3 **Not 'OO' or 'E' sound:** moor, wooden

Ⓕ 1 stoop
   2 shoot
   3 tooth
   4 noodle

Ⓖ

Note: UPPER and UTTER could also be placed the other way around.

Ⓗ 1 difficult
   2 grabbed
   3 upper
   4 taller
   5 different
   6 stiff
   7 unwell
   8 valley

Ⓘ 1 tall
   2 press
   3 up
   4 trip

Ⓙ 1 reduction
   2 portion
   3 decision
   4 creation
   5 mention
   6 rejection
   7 addition
   8 multiplication
   9 division
   10 position
   11 television
   12 collection
   13 version
   14 option
   15 caution
   16 question

Ⓚ 1 divide
   2 create
   3 multiply
   4 opt
   5 decide
   6 add
   7 collect
   8 reduce

Unit 8

Ⓐ **Across:**
   1 pigeon
   4 increase
   7 knowledge
   9 underwear
   10 netball
   11 treehouse
   12 rugby
   14 triplet
   15 undergrowth

   Down:
   1 pumpkin
   2 carefully
   3 wallpaper
   5 suppose
   6 often
   8 understand
   13 upon

Ⓑ **Any 5 of the following:**
   know + ledge = knowledge
   net + ball = netball
   of + ten = often
   pig + eon = pigeon
   pump + kin = pumpkin
   rug + by = rugby
   sup + pose = suppose
   tree + house = treehouse
   trip + let = triplet
   under + growth = undergrowth
   under + stand = understand
   under + wear = underwear
   up + on = upon
   wall + paper = wallpaper
   care + fully = carefully

Ⓒ
17	5	14	10	12	15	11	2	26	22	16	20	4	13	25	24	23	6	8
A	B	C	D	E	F	G	H	I	K	L	N	O	P	R	S	T	U	W

Ⓓ 1–3 Double 'S': chess, glass, guess
   4–8 Double 'L': retell, shrill, skull, stallion, telling
   9 Double 'F': giraffe
   10 Double 'E': cheese
   11–12 Double 'R': corridor, sparrow
   13–14 Double 'T': knitting, lettuce
   15 Double 'B': rabbit

(E) **1** sparrow   **2** chess   **3** knitting

(F) **Leftover letters spell:** GAMES AND SPORT VOCABULARY

(G) **Ball Games:** baseball, basketball, cricket, golf, hockey, rounders, snooker, squash, tennis
No Ball Games: judo, jumping, riding, running, swimming, athletics, badminton (Although badminton is a racquet sport it uses a shuttlecock instead of a ball).

(I) Accept any 10 correctly spelt words using these letters.
For example: am, as, clump, clumps, cup, cups, cusp, map, maps, maul, mauls, plum, plums, seal, seam, spam, sup, up

(J) **In any order:**
1 pleats   **2** staple   **3** pastel

Unit 9

(A) **Across:**

	Across:		Down:
2	trumpet	1	flesh
5	spider	2	thump
7	sting	3	chin
8	shirt	4	writing
9	skirt	6	drink
10	smack	7	spine
11	gloves	8	scarf
		9	shove
		12	swan

(B) **1** stung   **4** drank / drunk
2 flash / flush   **5** shave
3 short

(C) **1** cause – the reason something happens
2 cheek – part of the face
3 curtain – a fabric covering for a window
4 dairy – food such as milk, cheese, cream and yoghurt
5 diary – a little book with dates in it
6 diet – the food and drink that we eat
7 fairy – a little mythical creature with wings
8 fiery – very hot
9 flavour – the taste of something
10 fruit – food such as an apple, orange, pear or cherry
11 goose – a large bird
12 lion – an animal that roars and lives in groups called 'prides'
13 mainly – mostly
14 piano – a percussion musical instrument with a keyboard
15 saint – a person who has lived an especially religious life
16 toast – grilled bread

(D) **1** cause   **2** fiery   **3** mainly   **4** flavour

(E) **1** diet   **2** fiery   **3** lion   **4** cause

(F) **Leftover letters spell:** ALL OF THESE WORDS END WITH AL

(G) **1** petal   **5** festival
2 annual   **6** global
3 canal   **7** metal
4 hospital   **8** material

(H) **1** trousers   **9** lounge
2 brought   **10** course
3 curious   **11** count
4 youngest   **12** group
5 ought   **13** fought
6 various   **14** famous
7 countries   **15** pounce
8 would   **16** should

(I) **In any order:**
1 'OU – u': countries, famous, should, various, would
2 'OU – ow': count, lounge, pounce
3 'OU – or': brought, course, curious, fought

Unit 10

(A)

(B) **1** mount   **5** burned
2 burn   **6** experiment
3 chat / cant   **7** amount
4 mean / meat   **8** giant

(C) **1** meant   **5** burned
2 content   **6** experiment
3 disappoint   **7** amount
4 chant   **8** giant

(D) **1** confident   **3** content
2 disappoint   **4** distant

(E) **Across:**   **Down:**

	Across:		Down:
2	wagon	1	bacon
5	woman	3	guardian
6	certain	4	onion
7	potion	5	woken
9	women	8	salmon
10	sudden	9	widen
13	robin	11	urban
14	chicken	12	grain

(F)

20	6	16	13	8	21	10	14	22	5	15	19	18	11	25	23	4	1	7	9
A	C	D	E	F	G	I	K	L	M	N	O	P	R	S	T	U	V	W	Z

(G) **1** rifles   **4** surfaces   **7** sales
2 roses   **5** knives   **8** states
3 slices   **6** vines

(H) **1** calendar – an organiser of months and dates
2 cellar – an underground storage room
3 consider – to think about
4 farmer – someone who looks after cows, pigs and sheep
5 finger – a digit on our hands
6 guitar – a stringed musical instrument
7 manager – someone in charge
8 quartet – a group of four
9 remember – to not forget
10 similar – alike
11 sugar – a sweet additive
12 sweater – a jumper
13 teacher – someone who gives an education to pupils
14 teenager – someone between 13 and 19 years old
15 unclear – confused
16 vicar – someone who leads a church congregation

(I) **1** unclear   **7** guitar   **12** vicar
2 teenager   **8** sweater   **13** calendar
3 teacher   **9** teenager /   **14** cellar
4 calendar   manager   **15** consider
5 finger   **10** quarter   **16** farmer
6 teacher   **11** sweater

Unit 6

(A) All of the words in your list are made up of two shorter words. Divide your words into their two separate words. [15]

Example: sunbeam = _____*sun*_____ + _____*beam*_____

1 sunflower = _____ + _____

2 sunlight = _____ + _____

3 sunshine = _____ + _____

4 supply = _____ + _____

5 support = _____ + _____

6 tablet = _____ + _____

7 target = _____ + _____

8 teacup = _____ + _____

9 teapot = _____ + _____

10 teaspoon = _____ + _____

11 thinking = _____ + _____

12 toadstool = _____ + _____

13 toenail = _____ + _____

14 trapdoor = _____ + _____

15 teatime = _____ + _____

(B) Place one of your words in each space so that the sentences make sense. [9]

1 We gave my aunt some vintage crockery including a matching

_____ and _____ for her birthday.

2 Our _____ has grown really tall as it gets a good _____

of _____ and water.

3 I prefer to eat my ice cream with a _____ rather than a

dessert spoon.

4 I wrote a story about a fairy who lives under a _____ at the bottom

of the garden and uses a tiny _____ to get into our house and join

us at _____.

💡 **Helpful Hint**

Now you have split up your words, have a go at mixing them up to create some new compound words. **Example:** the word 'tea' could make 'teabag' and 'spoon' could make 'tablespoon'.

| sunbeam |
| sunflower |
| sunlight |
| sunshine |
| supply |
| support |
| tablet |
| target |
| teacup |
| teapot |
| teaspoon |
| teatime |
| thinking |
| toadstool |
| toenail |
| trapdoor |

24

Unit 6

blood

breed

broom

cooker

coop

deer

fleece

fool

foolish

gloomy

greet

indoors

keen

loop

sleeve

shoot

21

Ⓒ Change the double vowels in these words to make new words. [4]

Example: blood ____bleed____

1 deer _____ 3 breed _____

2 shoot _____ 4 fool _____

Ⓓ Put the letters of the following words in alphabetical order. [5]

Example: fleece ____c e e e f l____   3 greet _____

1 cooker _____ 4 sleeve _____

2 gloomy _____ 5 foolish _____

Ⓔ Place one of your words in each space so that the sentences make sense. [12]

1 A _____ is another word for an oven.

2 We can keep chickens in a _____.

3 I got some pasta sauce on my _____.

4 A _____ is an animal with antlers.

5 If we act daft, it means we are being _____.

6 The opposite of outdoors is _____.

7 We can brush the floor with a _____.

8 Our veins carry _____ around our body.

9 A miserable, dark room could be called _____.

10 We _____ friends when we say 'Hello!'

11 A poodle is a _____ of dog.

12 A _____ is a warm jacket.

 Helpful Hint

With double vowels we mostly double the 'o' or the 'e'. Some words such as 'aardvark' or 'skiing' will have other doubled vowels, but this is rare.

Unit 6

(F) All of these words are compound words. Use a line to join up two separate words that make up a compound word. [16]

| snow | moon | pass | out | rain | out | over | pack |

flake	all	bow	word	age	heard

standing	law	light	side	ball

take	port	way	coat	drop

| pass | rail | over | rain | snow | over | snow | out |

(G) It is common for the first part of a compound word to be a preposition, nature word, colour or body part. Divide your words into these three categories. Three have been done as examples. [13]

PREPOSITIONS	NATURE	OTHER
outlaw	*moonlight*	*package*

💡 **Helpful Hint**

Make sure that you know all of your prepositions as this will help you with compound word questions.

Unit 6 word list:

moonlight

outlaw

outside

outstanding

overall

overheard

overtake

package

passport

password

railway

rainbow

raincoat

snowball

snowdrop

snowflake

29

Unit 6

argue

build

business

definite

desperate

enough

especially

exercise

guide

particular

peculiar

perhaps

possession

separate

special

thought

20

(H) All of the words in your list are tricky to spell and sometimes little rhymes or mnemonics can help us to remember how to spell them. Work out which word each of these spelling aids helps with. [10]

1   There are four hissing snakes in this word. _____

2   The <u>Bus</u> number <u>1</u> visits the Loch <u>Ness</u> monster. _____

3   'I' 'C' 'U' in the middle of this word. _____

4   **G**uide **us** **i**n **d**ark **e**venings. _____

5   There is 'a rat' in this word. _____

6   **A r**ow **g**reatly **u**psets **e**veryone. _____

7   'C' I'm before **ALL** in this word. _____

8   Are 'U' a 'liar' at the end of this word? _____

9   'Th' symmetry around the letters OUG. _____

10   Spell me backwards from tail to head, I know Every **TIN I FED**. _____

(I) Use some of your words to fill in the grid below. One letter in each word has been provided as a clue. [10]

			P					
		O						
		S						
		S						
		E						
		S						
		S						
		I						
		O						
		N						

Helpful Hint

There will always be words that you find tricky to spell, but the best way of remembering a difficult word is to find a mnemonic or a rhyme to help you remember. The more creative your 'spelling aid' the more memorable it will be.

Unit 7

Ⓐ All of your words fit into the grid. Work out which number represents each letter to solve the puzzle. [18]

													4				
A	B	D	E	G	H	I	K	L	M	N	O	P	R	S	T	U	W	X

						7	4	4	10	8	11	25	26	4			9
		2	11	22	21						9		16				17
		7				16					16	17	16	11	25	26	4
		22				17			23		17		10				13
	2	26	23	9		22			26		16		26				14
		16				22			9		11		4				
7	19	16	17	22	22	7	20	25	10		25			22			
		10				20					26			17		23	
	10	26	22	13		25					4	10	8	11	25	26	4
		4			23	10	22	13						13		24	
														14			

Ⓑ Which of your words are synonyms for these words? [4]

1 vanish ____________

2 sunrise ____________

3 sunset ____________

4 unmanageable ____________

Ⓒ Which of your words are antonyms for these words? [6]

1 west ____________

2 possible ____________

3 wax ____________

4 north ____________

5 dawn ____________

6 unpopular ____________

Helpful Hint

Sometimes an opposite word uses a prefix such as 'im', 'in', 'dis' or 'ir'. When you see words beginning like this, work out the root of the word and you will have more of an idea as to the meaning of the whole word.

appear
dawn
disappear
dusk
east
impossible
irregular
north
popular
possible
regular
south
unpopular
wane
wax
west

28

Unit 7

creepy

flood

freezing

loose

meeting

moor

needle

noon

queen

sheet

smooth

spoon

steep

teeth

weekend

wooden

33

D Fill in the grid with all of your words. The first letter of each word has been given to help you. [16]

E Double vowels often change the sound of a word, for example two 'o's sound like 'oo'. Sort your words into the categories. Three have been done for you. [13]

oo	E	Not oo or E
noon	meeting	flood

F Change the double vowels in these words to make new words. [4]

1 steep _____

2 sheet _____

3 teeth _____

4 needle _____

💡 **Helpful Hint**

Always think about the sound before spelling a word. If the sound is 'E' the word is likely to have a 'magic e' on the end OR double 'e' OR 'ea' in the word. Now try writing down a word using these three ways and see if this helps you.

G Fill in the grid with all of your words. The first letter of each word has been given to help you. [16]

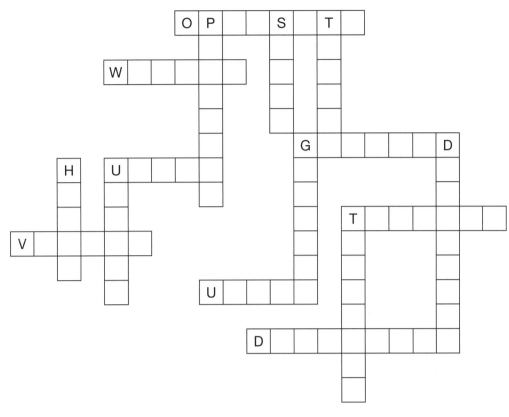

H Which of your words are antonyms for the following words? [8]

1   easy   _____   5   similar   _____

2   released   _____   6   loose   _____

3   lower   _____   7   healthy   _____

4   shorter   _____   8   hill   _____

I Write the root of these words below. [4]

Example: stiffer _____*stiff*_____

1   taller   _____   3   upper   _____

2   pressure   _____   4   tripping   _____

💡 **Helpful Hint**

When there are double consonants, check whether it is a double letter BEFORE a suffix and if so, remember our spelling rule: If a word ends in a SINGLE consonant and the letter before it is a SINGLE vowel, we double the last letter before adding our suffix. Following this rule will make the correct spelling most of the time.

Word list

different

difficult

grabbed

grammar

holly

opposite

pressure

stiff

taller

traffic

tripping

unwell

upper

utter

valley

warren

28

Unit 7

addition

caution

collection

creation

decision

division

mention

multiplication

option

portion

position

question

reduction

rejection

television

version

24

(J) Place one of your words in each space so that the sentences make sense. [16]

1   We save money because our school offers a _____ if we use their bookshop.

2   The pizza was divided so that we each had an equal _____ of it.

3   We had to make a _____ whether to buy a dog or a cat.

4   The baker's wedding cake was an amazing _____ .

5   Please don't _____ the secret party next weekend.

6   There was one _____ , but everyone else accepted our ideas.

7   Six plus two is an _____ sum.

8   Six times two is a _____ sum.

9   Six shared by two is a _____ sum.

10 We put the bird box in the best _____ : out of rain, sun and wind.

11 After my homework I can watch _____ for an hour.

12 Our library has a large _____ of local books.

13 We have the hardback _____ of that poetry book.

14 The pudding has the _____ of custard or cream.

15 _____ stops us running across the road without looking first.

16 The winner would be announced after the last _____ .

(K) Write the following words as verbs. [8]

Example: rejection ____*reject*____

1   division   _____   5   decision   _____

2   creation   _____   6   addition   _____

3   multiplication _____   7   collection   _____

4   option   _____   8   reduction   _____

 Helpful Hint

Words ending in 'tion' or 'sion' are often tricky. If the root word ends in 't' we use 'tion' and if the root word ends in 's' or 'd' we use 'sion'. This rule can sometimes be broken.

 Recap

 34

Unit 8

(A) Fill in the grid with all of your words, using the clues to help you. [16]

Across

1   Common town bird
4   To get bigger
7   Learning
9   An under layer of clothes
10 A ball game
11 A high-up playhouse
12 Game with an oval ball
14 One of three
15 Plants under trees

Down

1   Scary fruit
2   To take care
3   Covering for walls
5   Assume
6   Frequent
8   To know what to do
13 To be on

(B) Divide any five of your words into two separate words. [5]

Example: _____in_____ + _crease_ = _increase_

1   _____ + _____ = _____

2   _____ + _____ = _____

3   _____ + _____ = _____

4   _____ + _____ = _____

5   _____ + _____ = _____

carefully

increase

knowledge

netball

often

pigeon

pumpkin

rugby

suppose

treehouse

triplet

undergrowth

understand

underwear

upon

wallpaper

21

Unit 8

brass

cheese

chess

corridor

giraffe

glass

guess

knitting

lettuce

rabbit

retell

shrill

skull

sparrow

stallion

telling

36

C All of your words fit into the grid. Work out which number represents each letter to solve the puzzle. [18]

							22								
A	B	C	D	E	F	G	H	I	K	L	N	O	P	R	S	T	U	W

D Place your words into the correct groups. The first one has been done for you. [15]

Double 'S': *brass* 1 _____ 2 _____ 3 _____

Double 'L': 4 _____ 5 _____ 6 _____

7 _____ 8 _____

Double 'F': 9 _____   **Double 'E':** 10 _____

Double 'R': 11 _____ 12 _____

Double 'T': 13 _____ 14 _____

Double 'B': 15 _____

E Which of your words fit the following definitions? [3]

1 A small garden bird _____

2 A board game _____

3 Making things with needles and wool _____

Unit 8

F) All of your words are hidden in the word search. They go across and down but not diagonally. Find your words and then find the leftover letters. What do the leftover letters spell out? [17]

_____

B	A	D	M	I	N	T	O	N	T	E	N	N	I	S	G
A	A	M	R	O	U	N	D	E	R	S	R	E	S	A	C
S	W	I	M	M	I	N	G	N	S	Q	U	A	S	H	R
E	D	S	P	S	N	O	O	K	E	R	N	J	O	O	I
B	A	S	K	E	T	B	A	L	L	R	N	U	G	C	C
A	T	H	L	E	T	I	C	S	T	V	I	D	O	K	K
L	O	J	U	M	P	I	N	G	C	A	N	O	L	E	E
L	B	U	L	A	R	R	I	D	I	N	G	Y	F	Y	T

G) Can you divide your words up into 'ball' games and 'no ball' games? [16]

Ball Games	No Ball Games

Word list:

athletics

badminton

baseball

basketball

cricket

golf

hockey

judo

jumping

riding

rounders

running

snooker

squash

swimming

tennis

33

Unit 8

camp

cap

clamp

clap

claps

clasp

lamp

laps

lump

lumps

palms

saps

slam

slap

slump

spa

(H) An anagram is a word that can make another word if you rearrange the letters. All of the words in your list can be made out of the letters A, C, L, M, P, S and U. Find all of your words in the pyramid. You can move vertically, horizontally and diagonally and forwards or backwards. [16]

							C							
						A	M	P						
					C	L	A	M	P					
				A	P	C	L	A	P	S				
			C	L	A	S	P	C	L	A	P			
		L	A	P	S	P	L	U	M	P	S	A		
	P	A	L	M	S	A	P	S	L	U	M	P	S	
L	A	M	P	S	L	A	P	S	L	A	M	S	P	A
		S	L	U	M	P								

(I) Find another 10 words that use any mix of the following letters: A, C, L, M, P, S, E and U. [10]

1 _____   6 _____

2 _____   7 _____

3 _____   8 _____

4 _____   9 _____

5 _____   10 _____

(J) A clever tip to help solve anagrams is to place the letters of a word in a circle. What three words can these letters make? [3]

t

p   e

l   a

s

1 _____

2 _____

3 _____

29

Unit 9

A Fill in the grid with all of your words, using the clues to help you. [16]

Across

2   A musical brass instrument
5   An arachnid
7   A wasp or bee attack
8   An item of clothing with buttons
9   An item of clothing
10 To slap or hit
11 They keep our hands warm

Down

1   Skin
2   To punch
3   The bottom of our face
4   Using a pen or pencil
6   Liquid food
7   Our backbone
8   Item to keep your neck warm
9   To push or barge
12 A long-necked bird

B Change the vowel in the following words to make new words. [5]

Example: smack _____*smock*_____

1   sting _____   4   drink _____

2   flesh _____   5   shove _____

3   shirt _____

chin

drink

flesh

gloves

scarf

shirt

shove

skirt

smack

spider

spine

sting

swan

thump

trumpet

writing

Helpful Hint

Always sound out your words if they are tricky to spell. Words like these have double consonants to begin the words. A word such as 'writing' is tricky because of the silent 'w' but other words can be sounded out and this can help.

21

Unit 9

Bond SATs Skills Spelling and Vocabulary 9–10

cause

cheek

curtain

dairy

diary

diet

fairy

fiery

flavour

fruit

goose

lion

mainly

piano

saint

toast

24

C Draw a line to match each word with its definition. [16]

1	cause	A fabric covering for a window
2	cheek	Grilled bread
3	curtain	Foods such as milk, cheese, cream and yoghurt
4	dairy	Very hot
5	diary	A large bird
6	diet	A person who has lived an especially religious life
7	fairy	The reason something happens
8	fiery	Part of the face
9	flavour	A percussion musical instrument with a keyboard
10	fruit	A little book with dates in it
11	goose	A little mythical creature with wings
12	lion	Mostly
13	mainly	An animal that roars and lives in groups called 'prides'
14	piano	The food and drink that we eat
15	saint	The taste of something
16	toast	Food such as an apple, orange, pear or cherry

D Which of your words are synonyms for these words? [4]

1   reason _____   3   mostly _____

2   hot _____   4   taste _____

E Which of your words are antonyms for these words? [4]

1   binge _____   3   lioness _____

2   cool _____   4   effect _____

40

Unit 9

F) All of your words are hidden in the word search. They go across and down, but not diagonally. Find your words and then find the leftover letters. What do the leftover letters spell out? [17]

A	N	I	M	A	L	A	L	L	O	H	F
C	A	M	A	M	M	A	L	T	F	O	U
T	T	H	T	Y	P	I	C	A	L	S	N
U	U	P	E	E	S	E	W	O	O	P	N
A	R	E	R	C	A	N	A	L	R	I	A
L	A	T	I	R	D	S	E	N	A	T	T
D	L	A	A	M	E	T	A	L	L	A	U
W	I	L	L	T	G	L	O	B	A	L	R
F	E	S	T	I	V	A	L	H	A	L	A
C	A	S	U	A	L	A	N	N	U	A	L

G) Place one of your words in each space so that the sentences make sense. [8]

1   There was a ladybird sitting on the flower's _____.

2   Every February we have our _____ meeting.

3   Last summer we went boating on the Shropshire _____.

4   When I broke my leg I had an emergency x-ray at the local _____.

5   We went to a music _____ last summer.

6   I learnt about _____warming in science today.

7   We saw a historical suit of armour made out of _____ at the museum.

8   The guide explained that armour today still includes metal but is also made from other types of _____.

actual

animal

annual

canal

casual

festival

floral

global

hospital

mammal

material

metal

natural

petal

typical

unnatural

💡 **Helpful Hint**

Remember that words with an 'l' sound at the end can be spelt with 'le' (candle, angle), 'el' (gravel, angel) as well as 'al'. Sometimes writing down all three options can help you to recognise which ending makes the correct spelling.

25

brought

count

countries

course

curious

famous

fought

group

lounge

ought

pounce

should

trousers

various

would

youngest

28

(H) Place one of your words in each space so that the sentences make sense. [16]

1 Dad had a new pair of _____ for his birthday.

2 For the party I _____ the present and card with me.

3 I was _____ to find out what was in the other boxes.

4 My _____ child is only two years old.

5 I _____ to visit my aunt today as she is unwell.

6 There are _____ after-school clubs that we can join.

7 Greece, Poland and France are all _____ in Europe.

8 I never thought that he _____ break his leg just before the running race.

9 We waited in the hotel _____ until our taxi arrived.

10 We are doing a first-aid _____ at school next week.

11 The little boy could now _____ up to ten.

12 They are a friendly _____ that were on our coach.

13 The two brothers _____ over the television remote control.

14 My friend has a _____ cousin who sings in a well-known band.

15 The cat tried to _____ on the mouse but missed and skidded into the wall.

16 We _____ take an umbrella in case it rains.

(I) Write your words in the correct column so that each column of words has the same 'ou' sound. Three have been done as examples. [12]

OU – u	OU – ow	OU – or
youngest	*trousers*	*ought*

Unit 10

A Fill in the grid with all of your words. The first letter of each word has been given to help you. [16]

```
G  A  [ ] [ ]        D  [ ] [ ] [ ] [ ]
      [ ]            [ ]                    C
A  [ ] [ ] [ ]       [ ]                    [ ]
[ ]                  [ ]              R      [ ]
C  [ ] [ ] D  [ ] [ ]       R  [ ] [ ] [ ] [ ]
[ ]        [ ]              [ ]              [ ]
[ ]        [ ]    B  [ ]    S  [ ]           [ ]
[ ]     M  [ ]    [ ]       [ ]
[ ]     E  [ ] [ ] [ ] [ ]  [ ]
[ ]        [ ]    [ ]       [ ]
C  [ ] [ ] [ ] [ ]
         [ ] [ ]
```

B Remove one letter from each of the following words to make a new word. [4]

1 amount _____   3 chant _____

2 burnt _____   4 meant _____

C Which of your words are synonyms for these words? [8]

1 intended _____   5 scalded _____

2 happy _____   6 trial _____

3 let down _____   7 quantity _____

4 recite _____   8 massive _____

D Which of your words are antonyms for these words? [4]

1 shy _____   3 dissatisfied _____

2 amaze _____   4 near _____

accident

account

amount

burnt

chant

confident

content

decent

disappoint

distant

experiment

giant

meant

recent

rodent

spelt

32

43

Unit 10

bacon

certain

chicken

grain

guardian

onion

potion

robin

salmon

sudden

urban

wagon

widen

woken

woman

women

16

(E) Fill in the grid with all of your words, using the clues to help you. [16]

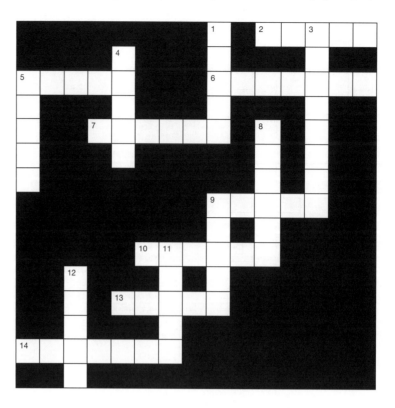

Across

2　A vehicle
5　A female adult
6　To be definite
7　A liquid with magical properties
9　More than one female adult
10　Quick
13　A garden bird
14　A hen

Down

1　Type of meat
3　Someone who looks after something
4　A vegetable
5　Interrupted from sleep
8　A fish
9　To make broader
11　Not rural
12　Cereal

💡 **Helpful Hint**

All of these words end in 'n', which is the second-most used consonant in the whole alphabet. The letter 'n' can come after every vowel, plus some consonants, when it comes at the end of a word. It also often has a silent letter in front of it. Why not give yourself one minute to think of as many words as you can that have 'n' as a starting letter, as an ending letter and as a middle letter in a word?

_____　　_____

_____　　_____

_____　　_____

_____　　_____

_____　　_____

F) All of your words fit into the grid. Work out which number represents each letter to solve the puzzle. [19]

				21																
A	C	D	E	F	G	I	K	L	M	N	O	P	R	S	T	U	V	W	Z	

amaze

awoke

compare

drove

else

grace

knife

programme

rifle

rose

sale

slice

state

surface

tame

vine

G) Write the plurals of these words. [8]

Example: programme _____*programmes*_____

1 rifle _____

2 rose _____

3 slice _____

4 surface _____

5 knife _____

6 vine _____

7 sale _____

8 state _____

💡 **Helpful Hint**

All of these words end in an 'e' which is the most common vowel ending in English. This often does the job of a 'magic e' which makes the previous vowel sound like its alphabet sound.

27

Unit 10

Bond SATs Skills Spelling and Vocabulary 9–10

calendar

cellar

consider

farmer

finger

guitar

manager

quartet

remember

similar

sugar

sweater

teacher

teenager

unclear

vicar

(H) Draw a line to match each word to its definition. [16]

1	calendar	Someone who gives an education to pupils
2	cellar	A group of four
3	consider	An organiser of months and dates
4	farmer	An underground storage room
5	finger	Someone who leads a church congregation
6	guitar	Someone between 13 and 19 years old
7	manager	To think about
8	quartet	Someone in charge
9	remember	A jumper
10	similar	Confused
11	sugar	Someone who looks after cows, pigs and sheep
12	sweater	A sweet additive
13	teacher	A stringed musical instrument
14	teenager	A digit on our hands
15	unclear	Alike
16	vicar	To not forget

(I) Which of your words have these smaller words hidden in them? [16]

1	ear _____		9	age _____
2	nag _____		10	art _____
3	tea _____		11	ate _____
4	end _____		12	car _____
5	fin _____		13	ale _____
6	her _____		14	cell _____
7	tar _____		15	con _____
8	eat _____		16	arm _____

32

Recap

46

Worked word searches

Unit 1

Ⓐ **Leftover letters spell:** WORDS WITH EA

Ⓕ **Leftover letters spell:** THESE WORDS ALL USE TH OR CH

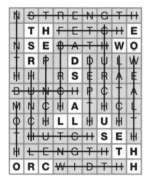

Unit 2

Ⓐ **Leftover letters spell:** WORDS THAT ARE FRUIT

Unit 3

Ⓗ **Leftover letters spell:** THESE ALL END IN A T

Unit 5

Ⓔ **Leftover letters spell:** COLOURFUL WORDS

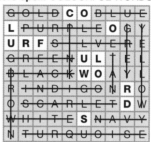

Unit 8

Ⓕ **Leftover letters spell:** GAMES AND SPORT VOCABULARY

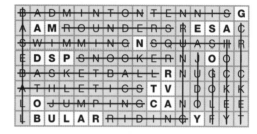

Ⓗ This is one possible solution.

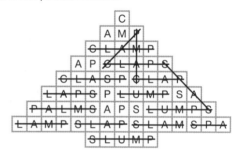

Unit 9

Ⓕ **Leftover letters spell:** ALL OF THESE WORDS END WITH AL

Progress chart

How did you do? Fill in your score below and shade in the corresponding boxes to compare your progress across the different tests and units.

50%   100%   50%   100%

Unit 1, p3 Score: __ / 31

Unit 1, p4 Score: __ / 30

Unit 1, p5 Score: __ / 28

Unit 1, p6 Score: __ / 26

Unit 2, p7 Score: __ / 27

Unit 2, p8 Score: __ / 25

Unit 2, p9 Score: __ / 32

Unit 2, p10 Score: __ / 33

Unit 3, p11 Score: __ / 35

Unit 3, p12 Score: __ / 22

Unit 3, p13 Score: __ / 28

Unit 3, p14 Score: __ / 31

Unit 4, p15 Score: __ / 28

Unit 4, p16 Score: __ / 20

Unit 4, p17 Score: __ / 32

Unit 4, p18 Score: __ / 26

Unit 5, p19 Score: __ / 21

Unit 5, p20 Score: __ / 27

Unit 5, p21 Score: __ / 24

Unit 5, p22 Score: __ / 30

Unit 6, p27 Score: __ / 24

Unit 6, p28 Score: __ / 21

Unit 6, p29 Score: __ / 29

Unit 6, p30 Score: __ / 20

Unit 7, p31 Score: __ / 28

Unit 7, p32 Score: __ / 33

Unit 7, p33 Score: __ / 28

Unit 7, p34 Score: __ / 24

Unit 8, p35 Score: __ / 21

Unit 8, p36 Score: __ / 36

Unit 8, p37 Score: __ / 33

Unit 8, p38 Score: __ / 29

Unit 9, p39 Score: __ / 21

Unit 9, p40 Score: __ / 24

Unit 9, p41 Score: __ / 25

Unit 9, p42 Score: __ / 28

Unit 10, p43 Score: __ / 32

Unit 10, p44 Score: __ / 16

Unit 10, p45 Score: __ / 27

Unit 10, p46 Score: __ / 32